'While engaged on this hunt I felt the earth move under my feet, and heard a soft big soughing sound, and looking round saw I had dropped in on a hippo banquet'

MARY KINGSLEY
Born 1862, London, England
Died 1900, Simonstown, South Africa

Selection taken from *Travels in West Africa*,
first published in 1897.

KINGSLEY IN PENGUIN CLASSICS
Travels in West Africa

MARY KINGSLEY

A Hippo Banquet

PENGUIN BOOKS

PENGUIN CLASSICS

UK | USA | Canada | Ireland | Australia
India | New Zealand | South Africa

Penguin Books is part of the Penguin Random House group of companies
whose addresses can be found at global.penguinrandomhouse.com.

This selection published in Penguin Classics 2015
002

Set in 9/12.4 pt Baskerville 10 Pro
Typeset by Jouve (UK), Milton Keynes
Printed in Great Britain by Clays Ltd, St Ives plc

A CIP catalogue record for this book is available from the British Library

ISBN: 978–0–141–39728–3

www.greenpenguin.co.uk

Penguin Random House is committed to a
sustainable future for our business, our readers
and our planet. This book is made from Forest
Stewardship Council® certified paper.

Contents

A Hippo Banquet

Tuesday, July 23rd. – Am aroused by violent knocking at the
door in the early gray dawn – so violent that two large centipedes and a scorpion drop on to the bed. They have
evidently been tucked away among the folds of the bar all
night. Well 'when ignorance is bliss 'tis folly to be wise,'
particularly along here. I get up without delay, and find
myself quite well. The cat has thrown a basin of water neatly
over into my bag during her nocturnal hunts; and when my
tea comes I am informed a man 'done die' in the night, which
explains the firing of guns I heard. I inquire what he has
died of, and am told 'He just truck luck, and then he die.'
His widows are having their faces painted white by sympa-
thetic lady friends, and are attired in their oldest, dirtiest
clothes, and but very few of them; still, they seem to be taking things in a resigned spirit. These Ajumba seem pleasant
folk. They play with their pretty brown children in a taking
way. Last night I noticed some men and women playing a
game new to me, which consisted in throwing a hoop at each
other. The point was to get the hoop to fall over your adversary's head. It is a cheerful game. Quantities of the common
house-fly about – and, during the early part of the morning,
it rains in a gentle kind of way; but soon after we are afloat
in our canoe it turns into a soft white mist.

We paddle still westwards down the broad quiet waters of

the O'Rembo Vongo. I notice great quantities of birds about here – great hornbills, vividly coloured kingfishers, and for the first time the great vulture I have often heard of, and the skin of which I will take home before I mention even its approximate spread of wing. There are also noble white cranes, and flocks of small black and white birds, new to me, with heavy razor-shaped bills, reminding one of the Devonian puffin. The hornbill is perhaps the most striking in appearance. It is the size of a small, or say a good-sized hen-turkey. Gray Shirt says the flocks, which are of eight or ten, always have the same quantity of cocks and hens, and that they live together 'white man fashion,' *i.e.*, each couple keeping together. They certainly do a great deal of courting, the cock filling out his wattles on his neck like a turkey, and spreading out his tail with great pomp and ceremony, but very awkwardly. To see hornbills on a bare sandbank is a solemn sight, but when they are dodging about in the hippo grass they sink ceremony, and roll and waddle, looking – my man said – for snakes and the little sand-fish, which are close in under the bank; and their killing way of dropping their jaws – I should say opening their bills – when they are alarmed is comic. I think this has something to do with their hearing, for I often saw two or three of them in a line on a long branch, standing, stretched up to their full height, their great eyes opened wide, and all with their great beaks open, evidently listening for something. Their cry is most peculiar and can only be mistaken for a native horn; and although there seems little variety in it to my ear, there must be more to theirs, for they will carry on long confabulations with each other across a river, and, I believe, sit up half the night and talk scandal.

There were plenty of plantain-eaters here, but, although their screech was as appalling as I have heard in Angola, they were not regarded, by the Ajumba at any rate, as being birds of evil omen, as they are in Angola. Still, by no means all the birds here only screech and squark. Several of them have very lovely notes. There is one who always gives a series of infinitely beautiful, soft, rich-toned whistles just before the first light of the dawn shows in the sky, and one at least who has a prolonged and very lovely song. This bird, I was told in Gaboon, is called *Telephonus erythropterus*. I expect an ornithologist would enjoy himself here, but I cannot – and will not – collect birds. I hate to have them killed any how, and particularly in the barbarous way in which these natives kill them.

The broad stretch of water looks like a long lake. In all directions sandbanks are showing their broad yellow backs, and there will be more showing soon, for it is not yet the height of the dry. We are perpetually grounding on those which by next month will be above water. These canoes are built, I believe, more with a view to taking sandbanks comfortably than anything else; but they are by no means yet sufficiently specialised for getting off them. Their flat bottoms enable them to glide on to the banks, and sit there, without either upsetting or cutting into the sand, as a canoe with a keel would; but the trouble comes in when you are getting off the steep edge of the bank, and the usual form it takes is upsetting. So far my Ajumba friends have only tried to meet this difficulty by tying the cargo in.

I try to get up the geography of this region conscientiously. Fortunately I find Gray Shirt, Singlet, and Pagan can speak trade English; for my interpreter's knowledge of that language seems confined to 'Praps,' ''Tis better so,' and 'Lordy, Lordy, helpee me' – a valueless vocabulary. None of them, however, seem to recognise a single blessed name on the chart, which is saying nothing against the chart and its makers, who probably got their names up from M'pongwes and Igalwas instead of Ajumba, as I am trying to. Geographical research in this region is fraught with difficulty, I find, owing to different tribes calling one and the same place by different names; and I am sure the Royal Geographical Society ought to insert among their 'Hints' that every traveller in this region should carefully learn every separate native word, or set of words, signifying 'I don't know,' – four villages and two rivers I have come across out here solemnly set down with various forms of this statement, for their native name. Really I think the old Portuguese way of naming places after Saints, &c., was wiser in the long run, and it was certainly pleasanter to the ears. My Ajumba, however, know about my Ngambi and the Vinue all right and Elivã z' Ayzingo, so I must try and get cross bearings from these.

We have an addition to our crew this morning – a man who wants to go and get work at John Holt's sub-factory away on the Rembwé. He has been waiting a long while at Arevooma, unable to get across, I am told, 'because the road is now stopped between Ayzingo and the Rembwé by "those fearful Fans."' 'How are we going to get through that way?' says I, with natural feminine alarm. 'We are not, sir,' says Gray Shirt. This is what Lady MacDonald would term a chatty little incident; and my hair begins to rise as I remember what I have been told about those Fans and the indications I have already seen of its being true when on the Upper Ogowé. Now here we are going to try to get through the heart of their country, far from a French station, and without the French flag. Why did I not obey Mr Hudson's orders not to go wandering about in a reckless way! Anyhow I am in for it, and Fortune favours the brave. The only question is: Do I individually come under this class? I go into details. It seems Pagan thinks he can depend on the friendship of two Fans he once met and did business with, and who now live on an island in Lake Ncovi – Ncovi is not down on my map and I have never heard of it before – anyhow thither we are bound now.

Each man has brought with him his best gun, loaded to the muzzle, and tied on to the baggage against which I am leaning – the muzzles sticking out each side of my head: the flint locks covered with cases, or sheaths, made of the black-haired skins of gorillas, leopard skin, and a beautiful bright bay skin, which I do not know, which they say is bush cow – but they call half a dozen things bush cow. These guns are not the 'gas-pipes' I have seen up north; but decent rifles which have had the rifling filed out and the locks replaced by flint locks and converted into muzzle loaders, and many of them have beautiful barrels. I find the Ajumba name for the beautiful shrub that has long bunches of red yellow and cream-coloured young leaves at the end of its branches is 'obãa.' I also learn that in their language ebony and a monkey have one name. The forest on either bank is very lovely. Some enormously high columns of green are formed by a

5

sort of climbing plant having taken possession of lightning-struck trees, and in one place it really looks exactly as if some one had spread a great green coverlet over the forest, so as to keep it dry. No high land showing in any direction. Pagan tells me the extinguisher-shaped juju filled with medicine and made of iron is against drowning – the red juju is 'for keep foot in path.' Beautiful effect of a gleam of sunshine lighting up a red sandbank till it glows like the Nibelungen gold. Indeed the effects are Turneresque to-day owing to the mist, and the sun playing in and out among it.

The sandbanks now have their cliffs to the N. N. W. and N. W. At 9.30, the broad river in front of us is apparently closed by sandbanks which run out from the banks thus: – yellow S. bank bright-red yellow N. bank. Current running strong along south bank. This bank bears testimony of this also being the case in the wet season, for a fringe of torn-down trees hangs from it into the river. Pass Seke, a town on north bank, interchanging the usual observations regarding our destination. The river seems absolutely barred with sand again; but as we paddle down it, the obstructions resolve themselves into spits of sand from the north bank and the largest island in mid-stream, which also has a long tail, or train, of sandbank down river. Here we meet a picturesque series of canoes, fruit and trade laden, being poled up stream, one man with his pole over one side, the other with his pole over the other, making a St Andrew's cross as you meet them end on.

Most luxurious, charming, and pleasant trip this. The men are standing up swinging in rhythmic motion their long, rich red wood paddles in perfect time to their elaborate melancholy, minor key boat song. Nearly lost with all hands. Sandbank palaver – only when we were going over the end of it, slipped sideways over its edge. River deep, bottom sand and mud. This information may be interesting to the geologist, but I hope I shall not be converted by circumstances into a human sounding apparatus again to-day. Next time she strikes I shall get out and shove behind.

We are now skirting the real north bank, and not the bank of an island or islands as we have been for some time here-tofore. Lovely stream falls into this river over cascades. The water is now rough in a small way and the width of the river great, but it soon is crowded again with wooded islands. There are patches and wreaths of a lovely, vermilion-flowering bush rope decorating the forest, and now and again clumps of a plant that shows a yellow and crimson spike of bloom, very strikingly beautiful. We pass a long tunnel in the bush, quite dark as you look down it – evidently the path to some native town. The south bank is covered, where the falling waters have exposed it, with hippo grass. Terrible lot of mangrove flies about, although we are more than one hundred miles above the mangrove belt. River broad again – tending W. S. W., with a broad flattened island with attributive sandbanks in the middle. The fair way is along the south bank of the river. Gray Shirt tells me this river is called the O'Rembo Vongo, or small River, so as to distinguish it from the main stream of the Ogowé which goes down past the south side of Lembarene Island, as well I know after that canoe affair of mine. Ayzingo now bears due north – and native mahogany is called 'Okooma.' Pass village called Welli on north bank. It looks

like some gipsy caravans stuck on poles. I expect that village
has known what it means to be swamped by the rising river;
it looks as if it had, very hastily in the middle of some night,
taken to stilts, which I am sure, from their present rickety
condition, will not last through the next wet season, and
then some unfortunate spirit will get the blame of the col-
lapse. I also learn that it is the natal spot of my friend
Kabinda, the carpenter at Andande. Now if some of these
good people I know would only go and distinguish themselves, I might write a sort of county family history of these
parts; but they don't, and I fancy won't. For example, the
entrance – or should I say the exit? – of a broadish little river
is just away on the south bank. If you go up this river – it
runs S. E. – you get to a good-sized lake; in this lake there
is an island called Adole; then out of the other side of the
lake there is another river which falls into the Ogowé main
stream – but that is not the point of the story, which is that
on that island of Adole, Ngouta, the interpreter, first saw the
light. Why he ever did – there or anywhere – Heaven only
knows! I know I shall never want to write his biography.

On the western bank end of that river going to Adole,
there is an Igalwa town, notable for a large quantity of fine
white ducks and a clump of Indian bamboo. My informants
say, 'No white man ever live for this place,' so I suppose the
ducks and bamboo have been imported by some black trader
whose natal spot this is. The name of this village is Wande-
regwoma. Stuck on sandbank – I flew out and shoved
behind, leaving Ngouta to do the balancing performances
in the stern. This O'Rembo Vongo divides up just below
here, I am told, when we have re-embarked, into three

streams. One goes into the main Ogowé opposite Ayshouka in Nkami country – Nkami country commences at Ayshouka and goes to the sea – one into the Ngumbi, and one into the Nunghi – all in the Ouroungou country. Ayzingo now lies N. E. according to Gray Shirt's arm. On our river there is here another broad low island with its gold-coloured banks shining out, seemingly barring the entire channel, but there is really a canoe channel along by both banks.

We turn at this point into a river on the north bank that runs north and south – the current is running very swift to the north. We run down into it, and then, it being more than time enough for chop, we push the canoe on to a sandbank in our new river, which I am told is the Karkola. I, after having had my tea, wander off. I find behind our high sand-bank, which like all the other sandbanks above water now, is getting grown over with hippo grass – a fine light green grass, the beloved food of both hippo and manatee – a forest, and entering this I notice a succession of strange mounds or heaps, made up of branches, twigs, and leaves, and dead flowers. Many of these heaps are recent, while others have fallen into decay. Investigation shows they are burial places. Among the *débris* of an old one there are human bones, and out from one of the new ones comes a stench and a hurrying, exceedingly busy line of ants, demonstrating what is going on. I own I thought these mounds were some kind of bird's or animal's nest. They look entirely unhuman in this desolate reach of forest. Leaving these, I go down to the water edge of the sand, and find in it a quantity of pools of varying breadth and expanse, but each surrounded by a rim of dark red-brown deposit, which you

9

can lift off the sand in a skin. On the top of the water is a film of exquisite iridescent colours like those on a soap bubble, only darker and brighter. In the river alongside the sand, there are thousands of those beautiful little fish with a black line each side of their tails. They are perfectly tame, and I feed them with crumbs in my hand. After making every effort to terrify the unknown object containing the food – gallant bulls, quite two inches long, sidling up and snapping at my fingers – they come and feed right in the palm, so that I could have caught them by the handful had I wished. There are also a lot of those weird, semi-transparent, yellow, spotted little sand-fish with cupshaped pectoral fins, which I see they use to enable them to make their astoundingly long leaps. These fish are of a more nervous and distrustful disposition, and hover round my hand but will not come into it. Indeed I do not believe the other cheeky little fellows would allow them to. They have grand butting matches among themselves, which wind up with a most comic tail fight, each combatant spinning round and going in for a spanking match with his adversary with his pretty little red-edged tail – the red rim round it and round his gill covers going claret-coloured with fury. I did not make out how you counted points in these fights – no one seemed a scale the worse.

The men, having had their rest and their pipes, shout for me, and off we go again. The Karkola soon widens to about 100 feet; it is evidently very deep here; the right bank (the east) is forested, the left, low and shrubbed, one patch looking as if it were being cleared for a plantation, but no village showing. A big rock shows up on the right bank, which is a change from the clay and sand, and soon the whole character of the landscape changes. We come to a sharp turn in the river, from north and south to east and west – the current very swift. The river channel dodges round against a big bank of sword grass, and then widens out to the breadth of the Thames at Putney. I am told that a river runs out of it here to the west to Ouroungou country, and so I imagine this Karkola falls ultimately into the Nazareth. We skirt the eastern banks, which are covered with low grass with a scanty lot of trees along the top. High land shows in the distance to the S. S. W. and S. W., and then we suddenly turn up into a broad river or straith, shaping our course N. N. E. On the opposite bank, on a high dwarf cliff, is a Fan town. 'All Fan now,' says Singlet in anything but a gratified tone of voice.

It is a strange, wild, lonely bit of the world we are now in, apparently a lake or broad – full of sandbanks, some bare and some in the course of developing into permanent islands by the growth on them of that floating coarse grass, any joint of which being torn off either by the current, a passing canoe, or hippos, floats down and grows wherever it settles. Like most things that float in these parts, it usually settles on a sandbank, and then grows in much the same way as our couch grass grows on land in England, so as to form a network, which catches for its adopted sandbank all sorts of floating *débris*; so the sandbank comes up in the world. The waters of the wet season when they rise drown off the grass; but when they fall, up it comes again from the root, and so gradually the sandbank becomes an island and persuades real trees and shrubs to come and grow on it, and its future is then secured.

We skirt alongside a great young island of this class; the sword grass some ten or fifteen feet high. It has not got any trees on it yet, but by next season or so it doubtless will have. The grass is stubbled down into paths by hippos, and just as I have realised who are the road-makers, they appear in person. One immense fellow, hearing us, stands up and shows himself about six feet from us in the grass, gazes calmly, and then yawns a yawn a yard wide and grunts his news to his companions, some of whom – there is evidently a large herd – get up and stroll towards us with all the flowing grace of Pantechnicon vans in motion. We put our helm paddles hard a starboard and leave that bank. These hippos always look to me as if they were the first or last creations in the animal world. At present I am undecided whether Nature tried 'her 'prentice hand' on them in her earliest youth, or whether, having got thoroughly tired of making the delicately beautiful antelopes, corallines, butterflies, and orchids, she just said: 'Goodness! I am quite worn out with this finicking work. Here, just put these other viscera into big bags – I can't bother any more.'

Our hasty trip across to the bank of the island on the other side being accomplished, we, in search of seclusion and in the hope that out of sight would mean out of mind to hippos, shot down a narrow channel between semi-island sandbanks, and those sandbanks, if you please, are covered with specimens – as fine a set of specimens as you could wish for – of the West African crocodile. These interesting animals are also having their siestas, lying sprawling in all directions on the sand, with their mouths wide open. One immense old lady has a family of lively young crocodiles running over her, evidently playing like a lot of kittens. The heavy musky smell they give off is most repulsive, but we do not rise up and make a row about this, because we feel hopelessly in the wrong in intruding into these family scenes uninvited, and so apologetically pole ourselves along rapidly, not even singing. The pace the canoe goes down that channel would be a wonder to Henley Regatta. When out of ear-shot I ask Pagan whether there are many gorillas, elephants, or bush-cows round here. 'Plenty too much,' says he; and it occurs to me that the corn-fields are growing golden green away in England; and soon there rises up in my mental vision a picture that fascinated my youth in the *Fliegende Blätter* representing 'Friedrich Gerstaecker auf der Reise.' That gallant man is depicted tramping on a serpent, new to M. Boulenger, while he attempts to club, with the butt end of his gun, a most lively savage who, accompanied by a bison, is attacking him in front. A terrific and obviously enthusiastic crocodile is grabbing the tail of the explorer's coat, and the explorer says 'Hurrah! das gibt wieder einen prächtigen Artikel für *Die Allgemeine Zeitung.*' I do not know where in the world Gerstaecker was at the time, but I should fancy hereabouts. My vigorous and lively conscience also reminds me that the last words a most distinguished and valued scientific friend had said to me before I left home was, 'Always take measurements, Miss Kingsley, and always take them from the adult male.' I know I have neglected opportunities of carrying this commission out on both those banks, but I do not feel like going back. Besides, the men would not like it, and I have mislaid my yard measure.

The extent of water, dotted with sandbanks and islands in

all directions, here is great, and seems to be fringed uniformly by low swampy land, beyond which, to the north, rounded lumps of hills show blue. On one of the islands is a little white house which I am told was once occupied by a black trader for John Holt. It looks a desolate place for any man to live in, and the way the crocodiles and hippo must have come up on the garden ground in the evening time could not have enhanced its charms to the average cautious man. My men say, 'No man live for that place now.' The factory, I believe, has been, for some trade reason, abandoned. Behind it is a great clump of dark-coloured trees. The rest of the island is now covered with hippo grass looking like a beautifully kept lawn. We lie up for a short rest at another island, also a weird spot in its way, for it is covered with a grove of only one kind of tree, which has a twisted, contorted, gray-white trunk and dull, lifeless-looking, green, hard foliage.

I learn that these good people, to make topographical confusion worse confounded, call a river by one name when you are going up it, and by another when you are coming down; just as if you called the Thames the London when you were going up, and the Greenwich when you were coming down. The banks all round this lake or broad, seem all light-coloured sand and clay. We pass out of it into a channel. Current flowing north. As we are entering the channel between banks of grass-overgrown sand, a superb white crane is seen standing on the sand edge to the left. Gray Shirt attempts to get a shot at it, but it – alarmed at our unusual appearance – raises itself up with one of those graceful preliminary curtseys, and after one or two preliminary flaps spreads its broad wings and sweeps away, with its long legs trailing behind it like a thing on a Japanese screen. Gray Shirt does not fire, but puts down his gun on the baggage again with its muzzle nestling against my left ear. A minute afterwards we strike a bank, and bang goes off the gun, deafening me, singeing my hair and the side of my face slightly. Fortunately the two men in front are at the moment in the recumbent position attributive to the shock of the canoe jarring against the cliff edge of a bank, or they would have had a miscellaneous collection of bits of broken iron pots and lumps of lead frisking among their vitals. It is a little difficult to make out how much credit Providence really deserves in this affair, but a good deal. Of course if It had taken the trouble to keep us off the bank, or to remind Gray Shirt to uncock his weapon, the thing would not have happened at all, but preliminary precaution is not Providence's peculiarity. Still, when the thing happened It certainly rose to it. I might have had the back of my head blown out, and the men might have been killed. I only hope this won't confirm Pagan permanently into superstition; for only a few minutes before, he had been showing me a big charm to keep him from being hurt by a gun. If he thinks about it, he will see there is nothing in the charm, because the other man who equally escaped was a charmless Christian.

The river into which we ran zig-zags about, and then takes a course S. S. E. It is studded with islands slightly higher than those we have passed, and thinly clad with forest. The place seems alive with birds; flocks of pelican and crane rise up before us out of the grass, and every now and then a crocodile slides off the bank into the water. Wonderfully like old logs they look, particularly when you see one letting himself roll and float down on the current. In spite of these interests I began to wonder where in this lonely land we were to sleep to-night. In front of us were miles of distant mountains, but in no direction the slightest sign of human habitation. Soon we passed out of our channel into a lovely, strangely melancholy, lonely-looking lake – Lake Ncovi, my friends tell me. It is exceedingly beautiful. The rich golden sunlight of the late afternoon soon followed by the short-lived, glorious flushes of colour of the sunset and the after-glow, play over the scene as we paddle across the lake to the N. N. E. – our canoe leaving a long trail of frosted silver behind her as she glides over the mirror-like water, and each stroke of the paddle sending down air with it to come up again in luminous silver bubbles – not as before in swirls of sand and mud. The lake shore is, in all directions, wreathed with nobly forested hills, indigo and purple in the dying daylight. On the N. N. E. and N. E. these come directly down into the lake; on N. W., N., S. W. and S. E. there is a band of well-forested ground, behind which they rise. In the north and north-eastern part of the lake several exceedingly beautiful wooded islands show, with gray rocky beaches and dwarf cliffs.

Sign of human habitation at first there was none; and in spite of its beauty, there was something which I was almost going to say was repulsive. The men evidently felt the same as I did. Had any one told me that the air that lay on the lake was poison, or that in among its forests lay some path to regions of utter death, I should have said – 'It looks like that'; but no one said anything, and we only looked round uneasily, until the comfortable-souled Singlet made the unfortunate observation that he 'smelt blood.' We all called him an utter fool to relieve our minds, and made our way towards the second island. When we got near enough to it to see details, a large village showed among the trees on its summit, and a steep dwarf cliff, overgrown with trees and creeping plants came down to a small beach covered with large water-washed gray stones. There was evidently some kind of a row going on in that village, that took a lot of shouting too. We made straight for the beach, and drove our canoe among its outlying rocks, and then each of my men stowed his paddle quickly, slung on his ammunition bag, and picked up his ready loaded gun, sliding the skin sheath off the lock. Pagan got out on to the stones alongside the canoe just as the inhabitants became aware of our arrival, and, abandoning what I hope was a mass meeting to remonstrate with the local authorities on the insanitary state of the town, came – a brown mass of naked humanity – down the steep cliff path to attend to us, whom they evidently regarded as an imperial interest. Things did not look restful, nor these Fans personally pleasant. Every man among them – no women showed – was armed with a gun, and they loosened their shovel-shaped knives in their sheaths as they came, evidently regarding a fight quite as imminent as we did. They drew up about twenty paces from us in silence. Pagan and Gray Shirt, who had joined him, held out their unembarrassed hands, and shouted out the name of the Fan man they had said they were friendly with: 'Kiva-Kiva.' The Fans stood still and talked angrily among themselves for some minutes, and then, Silence said to me, 'It would be bad palaver if Kiva no live for this place,' in a tone that conveyed to me the idea he thought this unpleasant contingency almost a certainty. The Passenger exhibited unmistakable symptoms of wishing he had come by another boat. I got up from my seat in the bottom of the canoe and leisurely strolled ashore, saying to the line of angry faces 'M'boloani' in an unconcerned way, although I well knew it was etiquette for them to salute first. They grunted, but did not commit themselves further. A minute after they parted to allow a fine-looking, middle-aged man, naked save for a twist of dirty cloth round his loins and a bunch of leopard and wild cat tails hung from his shoulder by a strip of leopard skin, to come forward. Pagan went for him with a rush, as if he were going to clasp him to his ample bosom, but holding his hands just off from touching the Fan's shoulder in the usual way, while he said in Fan, 'Don't you know me, my beloved Kiva? Surely you have not forgotten your old friend?' Kiva grunted feelingly, and raised up his hands and held them just off touching Pagan, and we breathed again. Then Gray Shirt made a rush at the crowd and went through great demonstrations of affection with another gentleman whom he recognised as being a Fan friend of his own, and whom he had not expected to meet here. I looked round to see if there was not any Fan from the Upper Ogowé whom I knew to go for, but could not see one that I could on the strength of a previous acquaintance, and on their individual merits I did not feel inclined to do even this fashionable imitation embrace. Indeed I must say that never – even in a picture book – have I seen such a set of wild wicked-looking savages as those we faced this night, and with whom it was touch-and-go for twenty of the longest minutes I have ever lived, whether we fought – for our lives, I was going to say, but it would not have been even for that, but merely for the price of them.

Peace having been proclaimed, conversation became general. Gray Shirt brought his friend up and introduced him to me, and we shook hands and smiled at each other in the conventional way. Pagan's friend, who was next introduced, was more alarming, for he held his hands for half a minute just above my elbows without quite touching me, but he meant well; and then we all disappeared into a brown mass of humanity and a fog of noise. You would have thought, from the violence and vehemence of the shouting and gesticulation, that we were going to be forthwith torn to shreds; but not a single hand really touched me, and as I, Pagan, and Gray Shirt went up to the town in the midst of the throng, the crowd opened in front and closed in behind, evidently half frightened at my appearance. The row when we reached the town redoubled in volume from the fact that the ladies, the children and the dogs joined in. Every child in the place as soon as it saw my white face let a howl out of it as if it had seen his Satanic Majesty, horns, hoofs, tail and all, and fled into the nearest hut, headlong, and I fear, from the continuance of the screams, had fits. The town was exceedingly filthy – the remains of the crocodile they had been eating the week before last, and piles of fish offal, and remains of an elephant hippo or manatee – I really can't say which, decomposition was too far advanced – united to form a most impressive stench. The bark huts are, as usual in a Fan town, in unbroken rows; but there are three or four streets here, not one only, as in most cases. The palaver house is in the innermost street, and there we went, and noticed that the village view was not in the direction in which we had come, but across towards the other side of the lake. I told the Ajumba to explain we wanted hospitality for the night, and wished to hire three carriers for to-morrow to go with us to the Rembwé.

For an hour and three-quarters by my watch I stood in the suffocating, smoky, hot atmosphere listening to, but only faintly understanding, the war of words and gesture that raged round us. At last the fact that we were to be received being settled, Gray Shirt's friend led us out of the guard house – the crowd flinching back as I came through it – to his own house on the right-hand side of the street of huts. It was a very different dwelling to Gray Shirt's residence at Arevooma. I was as high as its roof ridge and had to stoop low to get through the door-hole. Inside, the hut was four-teen or fifteen feet square, unlit by any window. The door-hole could be closed by pushing a broad piece of bark across it under two horizontally fixed bits of stick. The floor was sand like the street outside, but dirtier. On it in one place was a fire, whose smoke found its way out through the roof. In one corner of the room was a rough bench of wood, which from the few filthy cloths on it and a wood pillow I saw was the bed. There was no other furniture in the hut save some boxes, which I presume held my host's earthly possessions. From the bamboo roof hung a long stick with hooks on it, the hooks made by cutting off branching twigs. This was evidently the hanging wardrobe, and on it hung some few fetish charms, and a beautiful ornament of wild cat and leopard tails, tied on to a square piece of leopard skin, in the centre of which was a little mirror, and round the mirror were sewn dozens of common shirt buttons. In among the tails hung three little brass bells and a brass rattle; these bells and rattles are not only 'for dandy,' but serve to scare away snakes when the ornament is worn in the forest. A fine strip of silky-haired, young gorilla skin made the band to sling the ornament from the shoulder when worn. Gorillas seem well enough known round here. One old lady in the crowd outside, I saw, had a necklace made of sixteen gorilla canine teeth slung on a pineapple fibre string. Gray Shirt explained to me that this is the best house in the village, and my host the most renowned elephant hunter in the district.

We then returned to the canoe, whose occupants had been getting uneasy about the way affairs were going 'on top,' on account of the uproar they heard and the time we had been away. We got into the canoe and took her round the little promontory at the end of the island to the other beach, which is the main beach. By arriving at the beach when we did, we took our Fan friends in the rear, and they did not see us coming in the gloaming. This was all for the best it seems, as they said they should have fired on us before they had had time to see we were rank outsiders, on the apprehension that we were coming from one of the Fan towns we had passed, and with whom they were on bad terms regarding a lady who bolted there from her lawful lord, taking with her – cautious soul! – a quantity of rubber. The only white man who had been here before in the memory of man, was a French officer who paid Kiva six dollars to take him somewhere, I was told – but I could not find out when, or what happened to that Frenchman. It was a long time ago, Kiva said, but these folks have no definite way of expressing duration of time nor, do I believe, any great mental idea of it; although their ideas are, as usual with West Africans, far ahead of their language.

All the goods were brought up to my hut, and while Ngouta gets my tea we started talking the carrier palaver again. The Fans received my offer, starting at two dollars ahead of what M. Jacot said would be enough, with utter scorn, and every dramatic gesture of dissent; one man, pretending to catch Gray Shirt's words in his hands, flings them to the ground and stamps them under his feet. I affected an easy take-it-or-leave-it-manner, and looked on. A woman came out of the crowd to me, and held out a mass of slimy gray abomination on a bit of plantain leaf – smashed snail. I accepted it and gave her fish hooks. She was delighted and her companions excited, so she put them into her mouth for safe keeping. I hurriedly explained in my best Fan that I do not require any more snail; so another lady tried the effect of a pineapple. There might be no end to this, so I retired into trade and asked what she would sell it for. She did not want to sell it – she wanted to give it me; so I gave her fish hooks. Silence and Singlet interposed, saying the price for pineapples is one leaf of tobacco, but I explained I was not buying. Ngouta turned up with my tea, so I went inside, and had it on the bed. The door-hole was entirely filled with a mosaic of faces, but no one attempted to come in. All the time the carrier palaver went on without cessation, and I went out and offered to take Gray Shirt's and Pagan's place, knowing they must want their chop, but they refused relief, and also said I must not raise the price; I was offering too big a price now, and if I once rise the Fan will only think I will keep on rising, and so make the palaver longer to talk. 'How long does a palaver usually take to talk round here?' I ask. 'The last one I talked,' says Pagan, 'took three weeks, and that was only a small price palaver.' 'Well,' say I, 'my price is for a start to-morrow – after then I have no price – after that I go away.' Another hour how ever sees the jam made, and to my surprise I find the three richest men in this town of M'fetta have personally taken up the contract – Kiva my host, Fika a fine young fellow, and Wiki, another noted elephant hunter. These three Fans, the four Ajumba and the Igalwa, Ngouta, I think will be enough. Moreover I fancy it safer not to have an overpowering percentage of Fans in the party, as I know we shall have considerable stretches of unin-habited forest to traverse; and the Ajumba say that the Fans will kill people, *i.e.*, the black traders who venture into their country, and cut them up into neat pieces, eat what they want at the time, and smoke the rest of the bodies for future use. Now I do not want to arrive at the Rembwé in a smoked condition, even should my fragments be neat, and I am going in a different direction to what I said I was when leav-ing Kangwe, and there are so many ways of accounting for death about here – leopard, canoe capsize, elephants, &c. – that even if I were traced – well, nothing could be done then, anyhow – so will only take three Fans. One must diminish dead certainties to the level of sporting chances along here, or one can never get on.

No one, either Ajumba or Fan, knew the exact course we were to take. The Ajumba had never been this way before – the way for black traders across being *viâ* Lake Ayzingo, the way Mr Goode of the American Mission once went, and the Fans said they only knew the way to a big Fan town called Efoua, where no white man or black trader had yet been. There is a path from there to the Rembwé they knew, because the Efoua people take their trade all to the Rembwé. They would, they said, come with me all the way if I would guarantee them safety if they 'found war' on the road. This I agreed to do, and arranged to pay off at Hatton and Cookson's sub-factory on the Rembwé, and they have 'Look my mouth and it be sweet, so palaver done set.' Every load then, by the light of the bush lights held by the women, we arranged. I had to unpack my bottles of fishes so as to equalise the weight of the loads. Every load is then made into a sort of cocoon with bush rope.

I was left in peace at about 11.30 P. M., and clearing off the clothes from the bench threw myself down and tried to get some sleep, for we were to start, the Fans said, before dawn. Sleep impossible – mosquitoes! lice!! – so at 12.40 I got up and slid aside my bark door. I found Pagan asleep under his mosquito bar outside, across the doorway, but managed to get past him without rousing him from his dreams of palaver which he was still talking aloud, and reconnoitred the town. The inhabitants seemed to have talked themselves quite out and were sleeping heavily. I went down then to our canoe and found it safe, high up among the Fan canoes on the stones, and then I slid a small Fan canoe off, and taking a paddle from a cluster stuck in the sand, paddled out on to the dark lake.

It was a wonderfully lovely quiet night with no light save

that from the stars. One immense planet shone pre-eminent in the purple sky, throwing a golden path down on to the still waters. Quantities of big fish sprung out of the water, their glistening silver-white scales flashing so that they look like slashing swords. Some bird was making a long, low boom-booming sound away on the forest shore. I paddled leisurely across the lake to the shore on the right, and seeing crawling on the ground some large glow-worms, drove the canoe on to the bank among some hippo grass, and got out to get them.

While engaged on this hunt I felt the earth quiver under my feet, and heard a soft big soughing sound, and looking round saw I had dropped in on a hippo banquet. I made out five of the immense brutes round me, so I softly returned to the canoe and shoved off, stealing along the bank, paddling under water, until I deemed it safe to run out across the lake for my island. I reached the other end of it to that on which the village is situated; and finding a miniature rocky bay with a soft patch of sand and no hippo grass, the incidents of the Fan hut suggested the advisability of a bath. Moreover, there was no china collection in that hut, and it would be a long time before I got another chance, so I go ashore again, and, carefully investigating the neighbourhood to make certain there was no human habitation near, I then indulged in a wash in peace. Drying one's self on one's cummerbund is not pure joy, but it can be done when you put your mind to it. While I was finishing my toilet I saw a strange thing happen. Down through the forest on the lake bank opposite came a violet ball the size of a small orange. When it reached the sand beach it hovered along it to and

25

fro close to the ground. In a few minutes another ball of similarly coloured light came towards it from behind one of the islets, and the two waver to and fro over the beach, sometimes circling round each other. I made off towards them in the canoe, thinking – as I still do – they were some brand new kind of luminous insect. When I got on to their beach one of them went off into the bushes and the other away over the water. I followed in the canoe, for the water here is very deep, and, when I almost thought I had got it, it went down into the water and I could see it glowing as it sunk until it vanished in the depths. I made my way back hastily, fearing my absence with the canoe might give rise, if discovered, to trouble, and by 3.30 I was back in the hut safe, but not so comfortable as I had been on the lake. A little before five my men are stirring and I get my tea. I do not state my escapade to them, but ask what those lights were. 'Akom,' said the Fan, and pointing to the shore of the lake where I had been during the night they said, 'they came there, it was an "Aku"' – or devil bush. More than ever did I regret not having secured one of those sort of two phenomena. What a joy a real devil, appropriately put up in raw alcohol, would have been to my scientific friends!

Five Gorillas

I will not bore you with my diary in detail regarding our land journey, because the water-washed little volume attributive to this period is mainly full of reports of law cases, for reasons hereinafter to be stated; and at night, when passing through this bit of country, I was usually too tired to do anything more than make an entry such as: '5 S., 4 R. A., N. E. Ebony. T. I – 50, &c., &c.' – entries that require amplification to explain their significance, and I will proceed to explain.

Our first day's march was a very long one. Path in the ordinary acceptance of the term there was none. Hour after hour, mile after mile, we passed on, in the under-gloom of the great forest. The pace made by the Fans, who are infinitely the most rapid Africans I have ever come across, severely tired the Ajumba, who are canoe men, and who had been as fresh as paint, after their exceedingly long day's paddling from Arevooma to M'fetta. Ngouta, the Igalwa interpreter, felt pumped, and said as much, very early in the day. I regretted very much having brought him; for, from a mixture of nervous exhaustion arising from our M'fetta experiences, and a touch of chill he had almost entirely lost his voice, and I feared would fall sick. The Fans were evidently quite at home in the forest, and strode on over fallen trees and rocks with an easy, graceful stride. What saved us weaklings was the Fans' appetites; every two hours they sat down, and had a snack of a pound or so of meat and aguma apiece, followed by a pipe of tobacco. We used to come up with them at these halts. Ngouta and the Ajumba used to sit down; and rest with them, and I also, for a few minutes, for a rest and chat, and then I would go on alone, thus getting a good start. I got a good start, in the other meaning of the word, on the afternoon of the first day when descending into a ravine.

I saw in the bottom, wading and rolling in the mud, a herd of five elephants. I am certain that owing to some misapprehension among the Fates I was given a series of magnificent sporting chances, intended as a special treat for some favourite Nimrod of those three ladies, and I know exactly how I ought to have behaved. I should have felt my favourite rifle fly to my shoulder, and then, carefully sighting for the finest specimen, have fired. The noble beast should have stumbled forward, recovered itself, and shedding its life blood behind it have crashed away into the forest. I should then have tracked it, and either with one well-directed shot have given it its quietus, or have got charged by it, the elephant passing completely over my prostrate body; either termination is good form, but I never have these things happen, and never will. (In the present case I remembered, hastily, that your one chance when charged by several elephants is to dodge them round trees, working down wind all the time, until they lose smell and sight of you, then to lie quiet for a time, and go home.) It was evident from the utter unconcern of these monsters that I was down wind now, so I had only to attend to dodging, and I promptly dodged round a tree, thinking perhaps a dodge in time saves nine – and I lay down. Seeing they still displayed no emotion on my account, and fascinated by the novelty of the scene, I crept forward from one tree to another, until I was close enough to have hit the nearest one with a stone, and spats of mud, which they sent flying with their stamping and wallowing came flap, flap among the bushes covering me.

One big fellow had a nice pair of 40 lb. or so tusks on him, singularly straight, and another had one big curved tusk and one broken one. If I were an elephant I think I would wear the tusks straight; they must be more effective weapons thus but there seems no fixed fashion among elephants here in this matter. Some of them lay right down like pigs in the deeper part of the swamp, some drew up trunkfuls of water and syringed themselves and each other, and every one of them indulged in a good rub against a tree. Presently when they had had enough of it they all strolled off up wind, a way elephants have; but why I do not know, because they know the difference, always carrying their trunk differently when they are going up wind to what they do when they are going down — arrested mental development, I suppose. They strolled through the bush in Indian file, now and then breaking off a branch, but leaving singularly little dead water for their tonnage and breadth of beam. One laid his trunk affectionately on the back of the one in front of him, which I believe to be the elephant equivalent to walking arm-in-arm. When they had gone I rose up, turned round to find the men, and trod on Kiva's back then and there, full and fair, and fell sideways down the steep hillside until I fetched up among some roots.

It seems Kiva had come on, after his meal; before the

others, and seeing the elephants, and being a born hunter, had crawled like me down to look at them. He had not expected to find me there, he said. I do not believe he gave a thought of any sort to me in the presence of these fascinating creatures, and so he got himself trodden on. I suggested to him we should pile the baggage, and go and have an elephant hunt. He shook his head reluctantly, saying 'Kor, kor,' like a depressed rook, and explained we were not strong enough; there were only three Fans – the Ajumba, and Ngouta did not count – and moreover that we had not brought sufficient ammunition owing to the baggage having to be carried, and the ammunition that we had must be saved for other game than elephant, for we might meet war before we met the Rembwé River.

We had by now joined the rest of the party, and were all soon squattering about on our own account in the elephant bath. It was shocking bad going – like a ploughed field exaggerated by a terrific nightmare. It pretty nearly pulled all the legs off me, and to this hour I cannot tell you if it is best to put your foot into a footmark – a young pond, I mean – about the size of the bottom of a Madeira work arm-chair, or whether you should poise yourself on the rim of the same, and stride forward to its other bank boldly and hopefully. The footmarks and the places where the elephants had been rolling were by now filled with water, and the mud underneath was in places hard and slippery. In spite of my determination to preserve an awesome and unmoved calm while among these dangerous savages, I had to give way and laugh explosively; to see the portly, powerful Pagan suddenly convert himself into a quadruped, while Gray Shirt poised himself on one heel and waved his other leg in the air to advertise to the assembled nations that he was about to sit down, was irresistible. No one made such palaver about taking a seat as Gray Shirt; I did it repeatedly without any fuss to speak of. That lordly elephant-hunter, the Great Wiki, would, I fancy, have strode over safely and with dignity, but the man who was in front of him spun round on his own axis and flung his arms round the Fan, and they went to earth together; the heavy load on Wiki's back drove them into the mud like a pile-driver. However we got through in time, and after I had got up the other side of the ravine I saw the Fan let the Ajumba go on, and were busy searching themselves for something.

I followed the Ajumba, and before I joined them felt a fearful pricking irritation. Investigation of the affected part showed a tick of terrific size with its head embedded in the flesh; pursuing this interesting subject, I found three more and had awfully hard work to get them off and painful too for they give one not only a feeling of irritation at their holding-on place, but a streak of rheumatic-feeling pain up from it. On completing operations I went on and came upon the Ajumba in a state more approved of by Praxiteles than by the general public nowadays. They had found out about elephant ticks, so I went on and got an excellent start for the next stage.

By this time, shortly after noon on the first day, we had struck into a mountainous and rocky country, and also struck a track – a track you had to keep your eye on or you lost it in a minute, but still a guide as to direction.

The forest trees here were mainly ebony and great hard

wood trees, with no palms save my old enemy the climbing palm, *calamus*, as usual, going on its long excursions, up one tree and down another, bursting into a plume of fronds, and in the middle of each plume one long spike sticking straight up, which was an unopened frond, whenever it got a gleam of sunshine; running along the ground over anything it meets, rock or fallen timber, all alike, its long, dark-coloured, rope-like stem simply furred with thorns. Immense must be the length of some of these climbing palms. One tree I noticed that day that had hanging from its summit, a good one hundred and fifty feet above us, a long straight rope-like palm stem. Interested, I went to it, and tried to track it to root, and found it was only a loop that came down from another tree. I had no time to trace it further; for they go up a tree and travel along the surrounding tree-tops, take an occasional dip, and then up again.

The character of the whole forest was very interesting. Sometimes for hours we passed among thousands upon thousands of gray-white columns of uniform height (about 100–150 feet); at the top of these the boughs branched out and interlaced among each other, forming a canopy or ceiling, which dimmed the light even repetition of the equatorial sun to such an extent that no undergrowth could thrive in the gloom. The statement of the struggle for existence was published here in plain figures, but it was not, as in our climate, a struggle against climate mainly, but an internecine war from over population. Now and again we passed among vast stems of buttressed trees, sometimes enormous in girth; and from their far-away summits hung great bush-ropes, some as straight as plumb lines, others coiled round, and intertwined among each other, until one could fancy one was looking on some mighty battle between armies of gigantic serpents, that had been arrested at its height by some magic spell. All these bush-ropes were as bare of foliage as a ship's wire rigging, but a good many had thorns. I was very curious as to how they got up straight, and investigation showed me that many of them were carried up with a growing tree. The only true climbers were the *calamus* and the rubber vine (*Landolphia*), both of which employ hook tackle.

Some stretches of this forest were made up of thin, spindly stemmed trees of great height, and among these stretches I always noticed the ruins of some forest giant, whose death by lightning or by his superior height having given the demoniac tornado wind an extra grip on him, had allowed sunlight to penetrate the lower regions of the forest; and then evidently the seedlings and saplings, who had for years been living a half-starved life for light, shot up. They seemed to know that their one chance lay in getting with the greatest rapidity to the level of the top of the forest. No time to grow fat in the stem. No time to send out side branches, or any of those vanities. Up, up to the light level, and he among them who reached it first won in this game of life or death; for when he gets there he spreads out his crown of upper branches, and shuts off the life-giving sunshine from his competitors, who pale off and die, or remain dragging on an attenuated existence waiting for another chance, and waiting sometimes for centuries. There must be tens of thousands of seeds which perish before they get their chance; but the way the seeds of the hard wood African trees are packed, as it were, in cases specially made durable, is very wonderful.

Indeed the ways of Providence here are wonderful in their strange dual intention to preserve and to destroy; but on the whole, as Peer Gynt truly observes, '*Ein guter Wirth – nein das ist er nicht.*'

We saw this influence of light on a large scale as soon as we reached the open hills and mountains of the Sierra del Cristal, and had to pass over those fearful avalanche-like timber falls on their steep sides. The worst of these lay between Efoua and Egaja, where we struck a part of the range that was exposed to the south-east. These falls had evidently arisen from the tornados, which from time to time have hurled down the gigantic trees whose hold on the superficial soil over the sheets of hard bed rock was insufficient, in spite of all the anchors they had out in the shape of roots and buttresses, and all the rigging in the shape of bush ropes. Down they had come, crushing and dragging down with them those near them or bound to them by the great tough climbers.

Getting over these falls was perilous, not to say scratchy work. One or another member of our party always went through; and precious uncomfortable going it was I found, when I tried it in one above Egaja; ten or twelve feet of crashing creaking timber, and then flump on to a lot of rotten, wet *débris*, with more snakes and centipedes among it than you had any immediate use for, even though you were a collector; but there you had to stay, while Wiki, who was a most critical connoisseur, selected from the surrounding forest a bush-rope that he regarded as the correct remedy for the case, and then up you were hauled, through the sticks you had turned the wrong way on your down journey.

The Duke had a bad fall, going twenty feet or so before he found the rubbish heap; while Fika, who went through with a heavy load on his back, took us, on one occasion, half an hour to recover; and when we had just got him to the top, and able to cling on to the upper sticks, Wiki, who had been superintending operations, slipped backwards, and went through on his own account. The bush-rope we had been hauling on was too worn with the load to use again, and we just hauled Wiki out with the first one we could drag down and cut; and Wiki, when he came up, said we were reckless, and knew nothing of bush ropes, which shows how ungrateful an African can be. It makes the perspiration run down my nose whenever I think of it. The sun was out that day; we were neatly situated on the Equator, and the air was semi-solid, with the stinking exhalations from the swamps with which the mountain chain is fringed and intersected; and we were hot enough without these things, because of the violent exertion of getting these twelve to thirteen-stone gentlemen up among us again, and the fine varied exercise of getting over the fall on our own account.

When we got into the cool forest beyond it was delightful; particularly if it happened to be one of those lovely stretches of forest, gloomy down below, but giving hints that far away above us was a world of bloom and scent and beauty which we saw as much of as earth-worms in a flower-bed. Here and there the ground was strewn with great cast blossoms, thick, wax-like, glorious cups of orange and crimson and pure white, each one of which was in itself a handful, and which told us that some of the trees around us were showing a glory of colour to heaven alone. Sprinkled among them were

35

bunches of pure stephanotis-like flowers, which said that the gaunt bush-ropes were rubber vines that had burst into flower when they had seen the sun. These flowers we came across in nearly every type of forest all the way, for rubber abounds here.

I will weary you no longer now with the different kinds of forest and only tell you I have let you off several. The natives have separate names for seven different kinds, and these might, I think, be easily run up to nine.

A certain sort of friendship soon arose between the Fans and me. We each recognised that we belonged to that same section of the human race with whom it is better to drink than to fight. We knew we would each have killed the other, if sufficient inducement were offered, and so we took a certain amount of care that the inducement should not arise. Gray Shirt and Pagan also, their trade friends, the Fans treated with an independent sort of courtesy; but Silence, Singlet, the Passenger, and above all Ngouta, they openly did not care a row of pins for, and I have small doubt that had it not been for us other three they would have killed and eaten these very amiable gentlemen with as much compunction as an English sportsman would kill as many rabbits. They on their part hated the Fan, and never lost an opportunity of telling me 'these Fan be bad man too much.' I must not forget to mention the other member of our party, a Fan gentleman with the manners of a duke and the habits of a dustbin. He came with us, quite uninvited by me, and never asked for any pay; I think he only wanted to see the fun, and drop in for a fight if there was one going on, and to pick up the pieces generally. He was evidently a man of some importance, from the way the others treated him; and more-over he had a splendid gun, with a gorilla skin sheath for its lock, and ornamented all over its stock with brass nails. His costume consisted of a small piece of dirty rag round his loins; and whenever we were going through dense under-growth, or wading a swamp, he wore that filament tucked up scandalously short. Whenever we were sitting down in the forest having one of our nondescript meals, he always sat next to me and appropriated the tin. Then he would fill his pipe, and turning to me with the easy grace of aristocracy, would say what may be translated as 'My dear Princess, could you favour me with a lucifer?'

I used to say, 'My dear Duke, charmed, I'm sure,' and give him one ready lit.

I dared not trust him with the box whole, having a per-sonal conviction that he would have kept it. I asked him what he would do suppose I was not there with a box of lucifers; and he produced a bush-cow's horn with a neat wood lid tied on with tie, and from out of it he produced a flint and steel and demonstrated. Unfortunately all his grace's minor possessions, owing to the scantiness of his attire, were in one and the same pineapple-fibre bag which he wore slung across his shoulder; and these possessions, though not great, were as dangerous to the body as a million sterling is said to be to the soul, for they consisted largely of gunpowder and snuff, and their separate receptacles leaked and their contents, commingled, so that demonstra-tion on fire-making methods among the Fan ended in an awful bang and blow-up in a small way, and the Professor and his pupil sneezed like fury for ten minutes, and a cruel

37

world laughed till it nearly died, for twenty. Still that bag with all its failings was a wonder for its containing power.

The first day in the forest we came across a snake – a beauty with a new red-brown and yellow-patterned velvety skin, about three feet six inches long and as thick as a man's thigh. Ngouta met it, hanging from a bough, and shot backwards like a lobster, Ngouta having among his many weaknesses a rooted horror, of snakes. This snake the Ogowé natives all hold in great aversion. For the bite of other sorts of snakes they profess to have remedies, but for this they have none. If, however, a native is stung by one he usually conceals the fact that it was this particular kind, and tries to get any chance the native doctor's medicine may give. The Duke stepped forward and with one blow flattened its head against the tree with his gun butt, and then folded the snake up and got as much of it as possible into the bag, while the rest hung dangling out. Ngouta, not being able to keep ahead of the Duke, his Grace's pace being stiff, went to the extreme rear of the party, so that other people might be killed first if the snake returned to life, as he surmised it would. He fell into other dangers from this caution, but I cannot chronicle Ngouta's afflictions in full without running this book into an old-fashioned folio size. We had the snake for supper, that is to say the Fan and I; the others would not touch it, although a good snake, properly cooked, is one of the best meats one gets out here, far and away better than the African fowl.

The Fans also did their best to educate me in every way: they told me their names for things, while I told them mine, throwing in besides as 'a dash for top' a few colloquial phrases such as: 'Dear me, now,' 'Who'd have thought it,' 'Stuff, my dear sir,' and so on; and when I left them they had run each together as it were into one word, and a nice savage sound they had with them too, especially 'dearmenow,' so I must warn any philologist who visits the Fans, to beware of regarding any word beyond two syllables in length as being of native origin. I found several European words already slightly altered in use among them, such as 'Amuck' – a mug, 'Alas' – a glass, a tumbler. I do not know whether their 'Ami' – a person addressed, or spoken of – is French or not. It may come from 'Anwe' – M'pongwe for 'Ye,' 'You.' They use it as a rule in addressing a person after the phrase they always open up conversation with, 'Azuna' – Listen, or I am speaking.

They also showed me many things: how to light a fire from the pith of a certain tree, which was useful to me in after life, but they rather overdid this branch of instruction one way and another; for example, Wiki had, as above indicated, a mania for bush-ropes and a marvellous eye and knowledge of them; he would pick out from among the thousands surrounding us now one of such peculiar suppleness that you could wind it round anything, like a strip of cloth, and as strong withal as a hawser; or again another which has a certain stiffness, combined with a slight elastic spring, excellent for hauling, with the ease and accuracy of a lady who picks out the particular twisted strand of embroidery silk from a multi-coloured tangled ball. He would go into the bush after them while other people were resting, and particularly after the sort which, when split is bright yellow, and very supple and excellent to tie round loads.

On one occasion, between Egaja and Esoon, he came back from one of these quests and wanted me to come and see something, very quietly; I went, and we crept down into a rocky ravine, on the other side of which lay one of the outer most Egaja plantations. When we got to the edge of the cleared ground, we lay down, and wormed our way, with elaborate caution, among a patch of Koko; Wiki first, I following in his trail.

After about fifty yards of this, Wiki sank flat, and I saw before me some thirty yards off, busily employed in pulling down plantains, and other depredations, five gorillas: one old male, one young male, and three females. One of these had clinging to her a young fellow, with beautiful wavy black hair with just a kink in it. The big male was crouching on his haunches, with his long arms hanging down on either side, with the backs of his hands on the ground, the palms upwards. The elder lady was tearing to pieces and eating a pine-apple, while the others were at the plantains destroying more than they ate.

They kept up a sort of a whinnying, chattering noise, quite different from the sound I have heard gorillas give when enraged, or from the one you can hear them giving when they are what the natives call 'dancing' at night. I noticed that their reach of arm was immense, and that when they went from one tree to another, they squattered across the open ground in a most inelegant style, dragging their long arms with the knuckles downwards. I should think the big male and female were over six feet each. The others would be from four to five. I put out my hand and laid it on Wiki's gun to prevent him from firing, and he, thinking I was going to fire, gripped my wrist.

I watched the gorillas with great interest for a few seconds, until I heard Wiki make a peculiar small sound, and looking at him saw his face was working in an awful way as he clutched his throat with his hand violently.

Heavens! think I, this gentleman's going to have a fit; it's lost we are entirely this time. He rolled his head to and fro, and then buried his face into a heap of dried rubbish at the foot of a plantain stem, clasped his hands over it, and gave an explosive sneeze. The gorillas let go all, raised themselves up for a second, gave a quaint sound between a bark and a howl, and then the ladies and the young gentleman started home. The old male rose to his full height (it struck me at the time this was a matter of ten feet at least, but for scientific purposes allowance must be made for a lady's emotions) and looked straight towards us, or rather towards where that sound came from. Wiki went off into a paroxysm of falsetto sneezes the like of which I have never heard; nor evidently had the gorilla, who doubtless thinking, as one of his black co-relatives would have thought, that the phenomenon favoured Duppy, went off after his family with a celerity that was amazing the moment he touched the forest, and disappeared as they had, swinging himself along through it from bough to bough, in a way that convinced me that, given the necessity of getting about in tropical forests, man has made a mistake in getting his arms shortened. I have seen many

41

wild animals in their native wilds, but never have I seen anything to equal gorillas going through bush; it is a graceful, powerful, superbly perfect hand-trapeze performance.*

*   I have no hesitation in saying that the gorilla is the most horrible wild animal I have seen. I have seen at close quarters specimens of the most important big game of Central Africa, and with the exception of snakes, I run away from all of them; but although elephants, leopards and pythons give you a feeling of alarm, they do not give that feeling of horrible disgust that an old gorilla gives on account of its hideousness of appearance.

Elephant Hunt

I must now speak briefly on the most important article with which the Fan deals, namely ivory. His methods of collecting this are several, and many a wild story the handles of your table knives could tell you, if their ivory has passed through Fan hands. For ivory is everywhere an evil thing before which the quest for gold sinks into a parlour game; and when its charms seize such a tribe as the Fans, 'conclusions pass their careers.' A very common way of collecting a tooth is to kill the person who owns one. Therefore in order to prevent this catastrophe happening to you yourself, when you have one, it is held advisable, unless you are a powerful person in your own village, to bury or sink the said tooth and say nothing about it until the trader comes into your district or you get a chance of smuggling it quietly down to him. Some of these private ivories are kept for years and years before they reach the trader's hands. And quite a third of the ivory you see coming on board a vessel to go to Europe is dark from this keeping: some teeth a lovely brown like a well-coloured meerschaum, others quite black, and gnawed by that strange little creature – much heard of, and abused, yet little known in ivory ports – the ivory rat. This squirrel-like creature was first brought to Europe by Paul du Chaillu, and as far as I know no further specimen has been secured. I got two, but I am ashamed to say I lost them. Du Chaillu called it *Sciurus eborivorus*. Its main point, as may be imagined, is its teeth. The incisors in the upper jaw are long, and closely set together; those in the lower are still longer, and as they seem always to go in under the upper teeth, I wonder how the creature gets its mouth shut. The feet are hairless, and somewhat like those of a squirrel. The tail is long, and marked with transverse bars, and it is not carried over the back. Over the eyes, and on either side of the mouth, are very long stiff bristles. The mischief these little creatures play with buried ivory is immense, because, for some inscrutable reason, they seem to prefer the flavour of the points of the teeth, the most valuable part.

Ivory, however, that is obtained by murder is private ivory. The public ivory trade among the Fans is carried on in a way more in accordance with European ideas of a legitimate trade. The greater part of this ivory is obtained from dead elephants. There are in this region certain places where the elephants are said to go to die. A locality in one district pointed out to me as such a place, was a great swamp in the forest. A swamp that evidently was deep in the middle, for from out its dark waters no swamp plant, or tree grew, and evidently its shores sloped suddenly, for the band of swamp plants round its edge was narrow. It is just possible that during the rainy season when most of the surrounding country would be under water, elephants might stray into this natural trap and get drowned, and on the drying up of the waters be discovered, and the fact being known, be regularly sought for by the natives cognisant of this. I inquired carefully whether these places where the elephants came to die always had water in them, but they said no, and in one district spoke of a valley or round-shaped depression in among the mountains. But natives were naturally disinclined to take a stranger to these ivory mines, and a white person who has caught – as any one who has been in touch must catch – ivory fever, is naturally equally disinclined to give localities.

A certain percentage of ivory collected by the Fans is from live elephants, but I am bound to admit that their method of hunting elephants is disgracefully unsportsmanlike. A herd of elephants is discovered by rubber hunters or by dep-redations on plantations, and the whole village, men, women, children, babies and dogs turn out into the forest and stalk the monsters into a suitable ravine, taking care not to scare them. When they have gradually edged the elephants on into a suitable place, they fell trees and wreathe them very roughly together with bush rope, all round an immense enclosure, still taking care not to scare the elephants into a rush. This fence is quite inadequate to stop any elephant in itself, but it is made effective by being smeared with certain things, the smell whereof the elephants detest so much that when they wander up to it, they turn back disgusted. I need hardly remark that this preparation is made by the witch doctors and its constituents a secret of theirs, and I was only able to find out some of them. Then poisoned plantains are placed within the enclosure, and the elephants eat these and grow drowsier and drowsier; if the water supply within the enclosure is a pool it is poisoned, but if it is a running stream this cannot be done. During this time the crowd of men and women spend their days round the enclosure, ready to turn back any elephant who may attempt to break out, going to and fro to the village for their food. Their nights they spend in little bough shelters by the enclosure, watching more vigilantly than by day, as the elephants are more active at night, it being their usual feeding time. During the whole time the witch doctor is hard at work making incantations and charms, with a view to finding out the proper time to attack the elephants. In my opinion, his decision fundamentally depends on his knowledge of the state of poisoning the animals are in, but his version is that he gets his information from the forest spirits. When, however, he has settled the day, the best hunters steal into the enclosure and take up safe positions in trees, and the outer crowd set light to the ready-built fires, and make the greatest uproar possible, and fire upon the staggering, terrified elephants as they attempt to break out. The hunters in the trees fire down on them as they rush past, the fatal point at the back of the skull being well exposed to them.

When the animals are nearly exhausted, those men who do not possess guns dash into the enclosure, and the men who do, reload and join them, and the work is then completed. One elephant hunt I chanced upon at the final stage had taken two months' preparation, and although the plan sounds safe enough, there is really a good deal of danger left in it with all the drugging and ju-ju. There were eight elephants killed that day, but three burst through everything, sending energetic spectators flying, and squashing two men and a baby as flat as botanical specimens.

The subsequent proceedings were impressive. The whole of the people gorged themselves on the meat for days, and great chunks of it were smoked over the fires in all directions.

A certain portion of the flesh of the hind leg was taken by the witch doctor for ju-ju, and was supposed to be put away by him, with certain suitable incantations in the recesses of the forest; his idea being apparently either to give rise to more elephants, or to induce the forest spirits to bring more elephants into the district. Meanwhile the carcases were going bad, rapidly bad, and the smell for a mile round was strong enough to have taken the paint off a door. Moreover there were flies, most of the flies in West Africa, I imagine, and – but I will say no more. I thought before this experience that I had touched bottom in smells when once I spent the outside of a week in a village, on the sand bank in front of which a portly hippopotamus, who had been shot up river, got stranded, and proceeded energetically to melt into its elemental gases; but that was a passing whiff to this.

Fight with a Leopard

I must say the African leopard is an audacious animal, although it is ungrateful of me to say a word against him, after the way he has let me off personally, and I will speak of his extreme beauty as compensation for my ingratitude. I really think, taken as a whole, he is the most lovely animal I have ever seen; only seeing him, in the one way you can gain a full idea of his beauty, namely in his native forest, is not an unmixed joy to a person, like myself, of a nervous disposition. I may remark that my nervousness regarding the big game of Africa is of a rather peculiar kind. I can confidently say I am not afraid of any wild animal – until I see it – and then – well I will yield to nobody in terror; fortunately as I say my terror is a special variety; fortunately because no one can manage their own terror. You can suppress alarm, excitement, fear, fright, and all those small-fry emotions, but the real terror is as dependent on the inner make of you as the colour of your eyes, or the shape of your nose; and when terror ascends its throne in my mind I become preternaturally artful, and intelligent to an extent utterly foreign to my true nature, and save, in the case of close quarters with bad big animals, a feeling of rage against some unknown person that such things as leopards, elephants, crocodiles, &c., should be allowed out loose in that disgracefully dangerous way, I do not think much about it at the time. Whenever I have come across an awful animal in the forest and I know it has seen me I take Jerome's advice, and instead of relying on the power of the human eye rely upon that of the human leg, and effect a masterly retreat in the face of the enemy. If I know it has not seen me I sink in my tracks and keep an eye on it, hoping that it will go away soon. Thus I once came upon a leopard. I had got caught in a tornado in a dense forest. The massive, mighty trees were waving like a wheat-field in an autumn gale in England, and I dare say a field mouse in a wheat-field in a gale would have heard much the same uproar. The tornado shrieked like ten thousand vengeful demons. The great trees creaked and groaned and strained against it and their bush-rope cables groaned and smacked like whips, and ever and anon a thundering crash with snaps like pistol shots told that they and their mighty tree had strained and struggled in vain. The fierce rain came in a roar, tearing to shreds the leaves and blossoms and deluging everything. I was making bad weather of it, and climbing up over a lot of rocks out of a gully bottom where I had been half drowned in a stream, and on getting my head to the level of a block of rock I observed right in front of my eyes, broadside on, maybe a yard off, certainly not more, a big leopard. He was crouching on the ground, with his magnificent head thrown back and his eyes shut. His fore-paws were spread out in front of him and he lashed the ground with his tail, and I grieve to say, in face of that awful danger – I don't mean me, but the tornado – that depraved creature swore, softly, but repeatedly and profoundly. I did not get all these facts up in one glance, for no sooner did I see him than I ducked under the rocks, and remembered thankfully that leopards are said to have no power of smell. But I heard his observation on the weather, and the flip-flap of his tail on the ground. Every now and then I cautiously took a look at him with one eye round a rock-edge, and he remained in the same position. My feelings tell me he remained there twelve months, but my calmer judgment puts the time down at twenty minutes; and at last, on taking another cautious peep, I saw he was gone. At the time I wished I knew exactly where, but I do not care about that detail now, for I saw no more of him. He had moved off in one of those weird lulls which you get in a tornado, when for a few seconds the wild herd of hurrying winds seem to have lost themselves, and wander round crying and wailing like lost souls, until their common rage seizes them again and they rush back to their work of destruction. It was an immense pleasure to have seen the great creature like that. He was so evidently enraged and baffled by the uproar and dazzled by the floods of lightning that swept down into the deepest recesses of the forest, showing at one second every detail of twig, leaf, branch, and stone round you, and then leaving you in a sort of swirling dark until the next flash came; this, and the great conglomerate roar of the wind, rain and thunder, was enough to bewilder any living thing.

I have never hurt a leopard intentionally; I am habitually kind to animals, and besides I do not think it is ladylike to go shooting things with a gun. Twice, however, I have been in collision with them. On one occasion a big leopard had attacked a dog, who, with her family, was occupying a broken-down hut next to mine. The dog was a half-bred boarhound, and a savage brute on her own account. I, being roused by the uproar, rushed out into the feeble moonlight, thinking she was having one of her habitual turns-up with other dogs, and I saw a whirling mass of animal matter within a yard of me. I fired two mushroom-shaped native stools in rapid succession into the brown of it, and the meeting broke up into a leopard and a dog. The leopard crouched, I think to spring on me. I can see its great, beautiful, lambent eyes still, and I seized an earthen water-cooler and flung it straight at them. It was a noble shot; it burst on the leopard's head like a shell and the leopard went for bush one time. Twenty minutes after people began to drop in cautiously and inquire if anything was the matter, and I civilly asked them to go and ask the leopard in the bush, but they firmly refused. We found the dog had got her shoulder slit open as if by a blow from a cutlass, and the leopard had evidently seized the dog by the scruff of her neck, but owing to the loose folds of skin no bones were broken and she got round all right after much ointment from me, which she paid me for with several bites. Do not mistake this for a sporting adventure. I no more thought it was a leopard than that it was a lotus when I joined the fight. My other leopard was also after a dog. Leopards always come after dogs, because once upon a time the leopard and the dog were great friends, and the leopard went out one day and left her whelps in charge of the dog, and the dog went out flirting, and a snake came and killed the whelps, so there is ill-feeling to this day between the two. For the benefit of sporting readers whose interest may have been excited by the mention of big game, I may remark that the largest leopard skin I ever measured myself was, tail included, 9 feet 7 inches. It was a dried skin, and every man who saw it said, 'It was the largest skin he had ever seen, except one that he had seen somewhere else.'

The largest crocodile I ever measured was 22 feet 3 inches, the largest gorilla 5 feet 7 inches. I am assured by the missionaries in Calabar, that there was a python brought into Creek Town in the Rev. Mr Goldie's time, that extended the whole length of the Creek Town mission-house verandah and to spare. This python must have been over 40 feet. I have not a shadow of doubt it was. Stay-at-home people will always discredit great measurements, but experienced bushmen do not, and after all, if it amuses the stay-at-homes to do so, by all means let them; they have dull lives of it and it don't hurt you, for you know how exceedingly difficult it is to preserve really big things to bring home, and how, half the time, they fall into the hands of people who would not bother their heads to preserve them in a rotting climate like West Africa.